Registry of Guitar Tutors

GUITAR LESSONS

CHORD PLAYING

BY TONY SKINNER & ANDY DRUDY

A CIP record for this publication is available from the British Library.
ISBN: 1-898466-78-5

© 2005 Registry Publications Ltd

Lessons written by Tony Skinner; edited by Laurence Harwood.
Music composed by Tony Skinner; performed by Andy Drudy.
Music and text typesetting by Laurence Harwood.

Published by

Registry Mews, 11-13 Wilton Rd, Bexhill, E. Sussex, TN40 1HY

Printed and bound in Great Britain

CONTENTS

INTRODUCTION

This book contains ten lessons on chord playing techniques, and has been designed to be used both by tutors and students of the guitar. Tutors will find the book extremely effective as a teaching aid, as it contains ready-made lessons through which pupils can be guided.

Students will find that the lessons are presented in an accessible and informative manner, and that by listening to, and playing along with, the examples on the CD their playing will quickly improve.

How To Use This Book

Each lesson consists of the main lesson text, followed by several musical examples in both music notation and tablature. The musical examples are all demonstrated on the accompanying CD. The CD track relevant to the example is shown above the notation with this symbol: ⊙ **5** – e.g. track 5 on the CD.

Backing tracks for many of the examples are also included on the CD, so that the reader can play along with a musical accompaniment. The CD track number is given above the examples with backing tracks.

A tuning guide is provided on track 1 of the CD.

REGISTRY OF GUITAR TUTORS

This book was written by Tony Skinner, Director of the Registry Of Guitar Tutors

The Registry Of Guitar Tutors (RGT) is the world's foremost organisation for guitar education. RGT has a membership of thousands of registered guitar tutors, not only in the UK but also in many countries across the world.

Gain A Guitar Playing Qualification

RGT compiles examinations in electric, acoustic, bass and classical guitar – from beginner to diploma level. These are organised in partnership with London College of Music Examinations, one of the world's leading music examination boards. The examinations are accredited by the Qualifications and Curriculum Authority (QCA) and, for higher grades, also by the Universities and Colleges Admissions Service (UCAS).

You can study for an RGT exam from home with a course handbook, or via lessons with a local tutor. (Contact the RGT if you need to find a registered guitar tutor in your area.)

Studying for an RGT examination will help you develop your guitar playing in a structured and comprehensive way. To find out which level exam grade your playing is at, view the RGT website www.RegistryOfGuitarTutors.com or call the RGT for a free exam information pack on 01424 222222 (or 0044 1424 222222 from outside the UK).

NOTATION GUIDE

All of the music examples in this book are written in both traditional music notation and tablature (TAB).

MUSIC NOTATION

Music for the guitar is traditionally written using the treble clef. The illustration below shows a range of notes on the treble clef – from the low open E string to the 12th fret on the high E string.

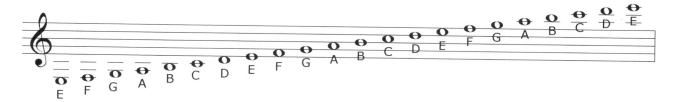

A sharp (♯) before a note would raise its pitch by a semitone (i.e. one fret higher), whilst a flat (♭) before a note would lower its pitch by a semitone (i.e. one fret lower). A natural sign (x) before a note cancels a sharp or flat sign.

TABLATURE

TAB is a system of notating guitar music that uses horizontal lines to represent the strings – with the top line representing the high E (1st) string and the bottom line representing the low E (6th) string.

Numbers on the lines indicate the fret number. A zero on a line indicates that the string should be played open (i.e. unfretted).

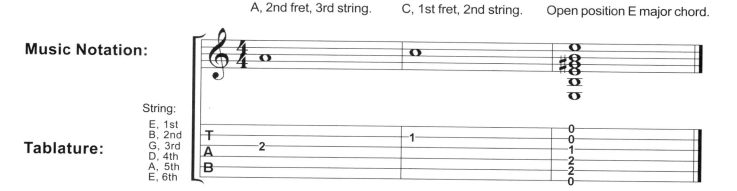

READING RESOURCES

If you need help in reading music notation, a wide range of sight-reading books specifically for guitarists is available at:

www.BooksForGuitar.com

Notation Symbols

Hammer-on & Pull-off

Hammer-on (H): Pick the first note, then sound the higher note by fretting without picking. Pull-off (P): Pick the first note, then sound the lower note by pulling finger off string.

Slide

Pick the first note, then, whilst keeping pressure on the fingerboard, move down (or up) to the note indicated.

Accent

Accentuate the note or chord indicated.

Picking Direction

⊓ = Downstroke
V = Upstroke

Arpeggiated Chord

Bring out the individual notes in a chord by strumming across the strings in the direction indicated.

Staccato

The note is played short and detached.

Repeat Directions

Repeat from beginning.

Repeat music between 'double dot' signs.

On the first repeat, play the first bracketed section; on the second repeat play the second section instead. 'D.C.' means play again from the beginning.

Repeat the previous bar.

Repeat the previous two bars.

Other Performance Directions

L.V. - Allow strings to ring.

Tacet - Do not play.

CHANGING CHORDS

IT IS ONE THING TO KNOW YOUR CHORD SHAPES, BUT IT IS ANOTHER, FAR MORE USEFUL, SKILL TO BE ABLE TO CHANGE FLUENTLY BETWEEN THEM.

Leaving gaps between chords when strumming through a song or chord progression will result in a fragmented sounding performance and will also make it hard to keep in time – therefore it is essential that chord changes are crisp and prompt. This might not be too hard when using chords that you are very familiar with, but it can seem daunting with chords that are new to you. However, changing between any chords can be made much easier if you follow the 'minimum movement principle'. As the name suggests, this involves making only the smallest finger movements necessary when moving between chords, and avoiding taking fingers off strings or frets only to put them back on again for the next chord. Excess movement between chords is what slows chord changes down: the less your fingers move the faster your chord changes will be.

STAYING PUT

If you look carefully at the fingering for various chords you may notice that some chords have one or more notes in common. For example, the open position Am and D7 chords both include the note C (first fret on the B string). The C major chord also includes this note and in addition has another note in common with the Am chord (E on the 2nd fret of the D string). The chord progression shown in exercise 1 (CD tracks 2 & 3) uses the chords Am, D7, C and E: notice the common fingering between each chord change; in particular, how the first finger stays on the first fret and how the second finger stays on the second fret throughout.

Some guitarists make a musical feature of this technique, by keeping some fingers on particular notes whilst the underlying chord shapes change. This has the double benefit of making the chord progression sound more interesting, yet at the same time it is actually easier to play than using standard chord shapes: a win-win situation! An example is given in exercise 2 (CD tracks 4 & 5).

SPOTTING LINKS

Even if different chords do not contain too many common notes, changing between them can still be made easier if you look out for any relationships and visual links between them. For example, in exercise 3 (CD tracks 6 & 7), when changing between the B7 and A major chords the first finger can be slid along the fourth string (between frets one and two) rather than being taken off the string only to be put back on a fret higher a moment later. Following this 'minimum movement principle' saves time and makes chord changes much smoother. No matter how seemingly remote a chord change is, there will always be some kind of link between the chords that, once spotted, will make changing between them easier. However, if all else fails, there is a little trick you can use that will mask any gap between chord changes: using an 'open vamp'. This simply involves strumming the open strings whilst your fingers move between the chord change – whilst not ideal, it does mean that the overall fluency and momentum of the performance is maintained. In fact, some players actually make a feature of this technique to bring out accents within their rhythm playing. Exercise 4 is an example of this useful technique (CD tracks 8 & 9). Whatever technique you use, the golden rule in rhythm playing is 'never stop – always keep strumming'.

Exercise 1: Chord Sequence 1 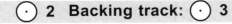 2　Backing track: 3

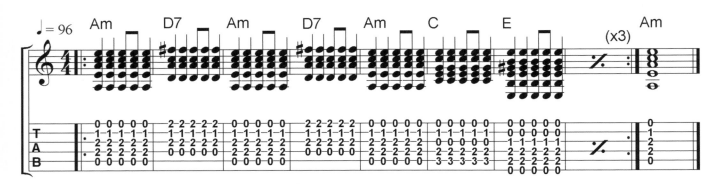

Between Am and D7 keep the first finger on the first fret of the second string, and just move the second and third fingers across the strings. Between Am and C only move the third finger, keeping the others in place. Notice how E major is the same 'shape' as Am – just on different strings.

Exercise 2: Chord Sequence 2 4　Backing track: 5

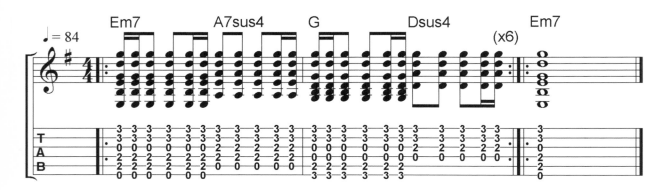

In this progression the third and fourth fingers remain in the same position throughout all the chord changes. Do not be tempted to lift them off at any point.

Exercise 3: Chord Sequence 3 6　Backing track: 7

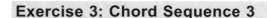

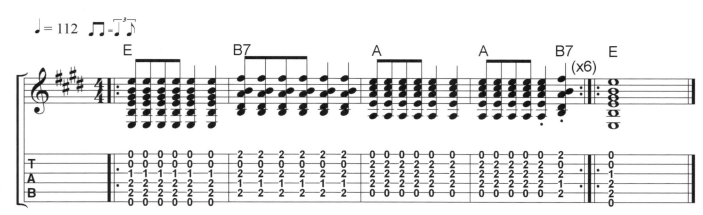

In this folky progression it's important to spot the common links between consecutive chord shapes. For example, between E and B7 the second finger should stay on the second fret of the fifth string.

Exercise 4: Chord Sequence 4

8   **Backing track:** 9

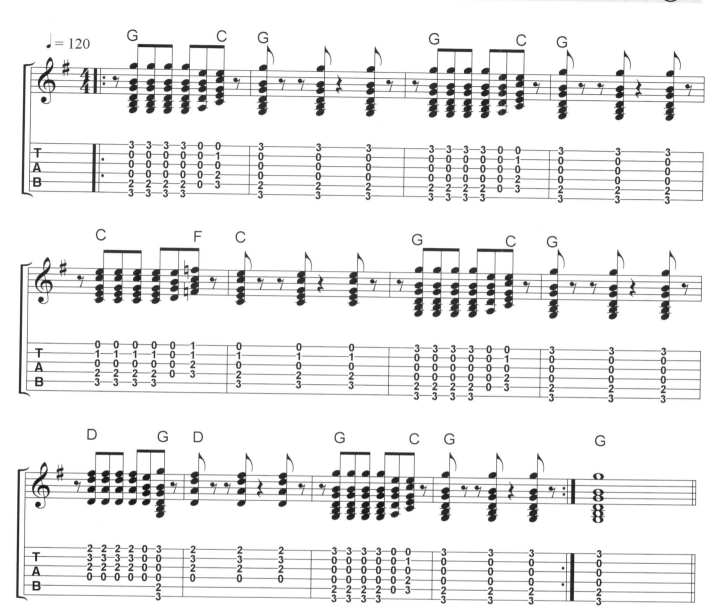

In this progression the chord changes are quite fast, but they are made much easier by using an open string vamp between each chord. Strumming the open strings between each chord gives you a little breathing space to move your fingers onto the next chord shape.

Technique tip

Be careful not to over-grip with the fretting-hand thumb on the back of the neck as this will cause muscle fatigue and tend to limit freedom of the thumb to move. It is essential that the fretting-hand thumb is allowed to move freely when changing chords: if the thumb remains static this restricts the optimum positioning of the fingers for the next chord, which may result in unnecessary stretching and the involuntary dampening of certain strings (as the fingers are not positioned upright on their tips). Be aware that for the fingers to move freely the wrist, elbow and shoulder must be flexible and relaxed: try to ensure that this is not inhibited by your standing or sitting position.

LESSON ONE – CHANGING CHORDS   9

STRUMMING PATTERNS

AS A MEMBER OF A BAND, YOU'LL PROBABLY SPEND MORE TIME PLAYING RHYTHM GUITAR THAN LEAD. GET STARTED WITH THESE CLASSIC STRUMMING PATTERNS.

Rhythm guitar playing rarely gains as much attention as lead playing, but it should be remembered that rhythm playing forms the backbone of most songs. Developing a reliable and inventive strumming technique is a vital part of becoming a good guitar player.

ESSENTIAL SKILLS

The most essential skill required to become a good rhythm player is the ability to play in time: practising with a metronome, drum machine or the CD backing tracks with this book, will provide the ideal preparation; always listen out for the drums and bass and try to stay in time with them. Another core skill is the ability to change fluently from one chord to another: always look for links, or common notes, between consecutive chords - these will help you make chord changes smooth and unnoticeable. (This is covered in more detail in the previous lesson, 'Changing Chords'). Once you have mastered these basic rhythm playing skills, it is time to become inventive with your strumming patterns. It is the uniqueness and inventiveness of strumming that distinguishes great rhythm players from the rest.

TECHNIQUE

To develop a good strumming technique, make sure that the strumming action comes from the wrist: if you fail to do this, and keep the wrist tight and strum using the whole forearm, you will severely restrict the potential speed and fluency of your rhythm playing. Practise in front of a mirror, or video yourself, so that you can see if you are using the right technique.

In the following strumming exercises, you will gain the most benefit if you start by playing all the progressions through using just four downstrums per bar – this way you will become familiar with the chord changes before tackling the strumming patterns. Although all the chords are notated in full, there is no need to necessarily strum all the strings on every beat – feel free to add variety, particularly by omitting some bass strings on upstrokes, and some treble strings on downstokes.

Exercise 1: Rhythm Using An Upstroke   ⊙ 10

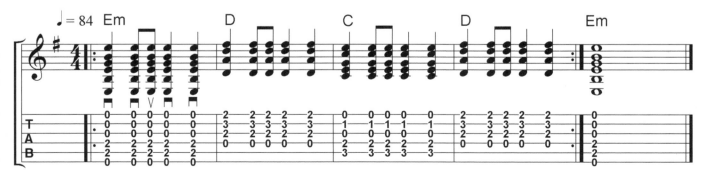

This simple pattern uses four downstrums per bar, with rhythmic interest being created by the use of an upstroke after the second beat.

Exercise 2: Rhythm Using Accents

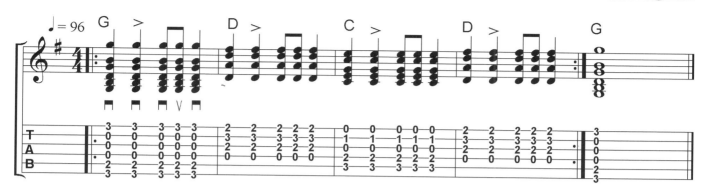

The second beat of the bar is accented to create dynamic variety. An upstroke is used after the third beat of the bar.

Exercise 3: Rhythm Using Open String Vamps

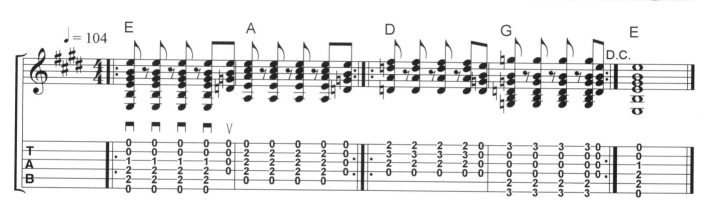

This pattern uses four downstrums per bar, with an open string upstroke vamp at the end of each bar. The open string vamp is used to create rhythmic interest, but it also makes changing to the next chord much easier. The D.C. symbol means play, the complete 8-bar progression, again from the beginning, before ending on E major.

Exercise 4: Rhythm Using Sustained Chord

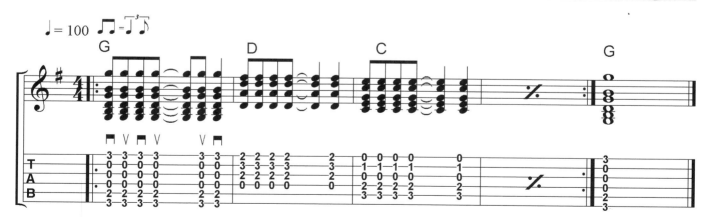

This pattern uses a mixture of down and upstrokes, but notice how the fourth strum is held longer than the others. This variety creates an effective rhythm.

Exercise 5: Rhythm Using Rests

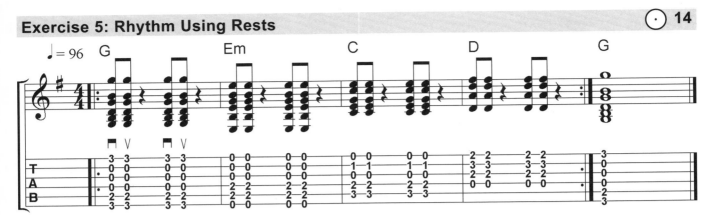

A simple down-up strum pattern, but the use of rests creates a very distinctive rhythmic effect.

Exercise 6: Rhythm Using Variations

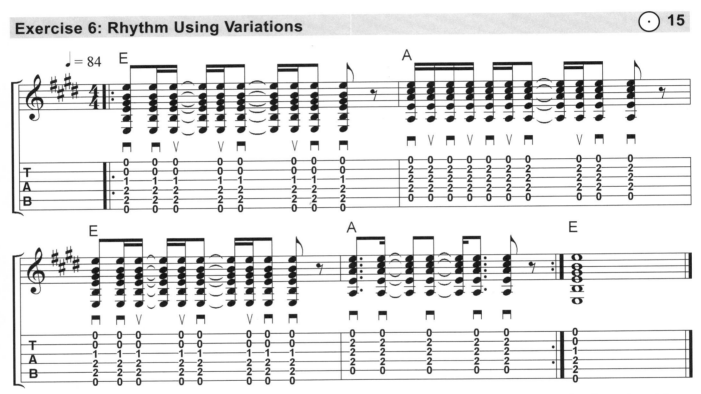

This 'Bo Diddley' type pattern is a good example of how to use rhythmic variations: notice that bars 1 and 3 are the same, whilst bars 2 and 4 are each variations on the first bar.

Exercise 7: Rhythm Using Pre-Strums

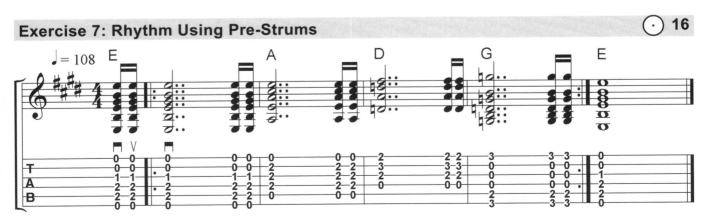

This typical rock strumming pattern is essentially just one strum per bar. What makes it distinctive is the rapid down-up 'pre-strum' before the main beat. These 'pre-strums' do not need to be played across all the strings, and open strings can be used on the second of them to help get to the main chord quickly.

CHORD VARIATIONS

BY VARYING THE FINGERING FOR SOME OF THE MOST BASIC CHORDS YOU CAN DISCOVER SOME REALLY GREAT SOUNDING CHORD EMBELLISHMENTS.

Chord embellishment consists of taking a chord and varying it: either by substituting a note within it for a new note, or by adding a note to the existing notes of the chord. Whichever method is used, the new note should be taken from the 'key scale' of the chord: for example, you could add any note of the C major scale to the C major chord without changing the fundamental harmonic nature of the chord. By sticking to notes from the key scale the new embellished chord can normally be used as a direct replacement for the simpler basic chord – without causing any clashes with the melody of the song. However, if you choose to use notes from outside the key scale then the harmonic nature of the chord will be changed (e.g. a major chord might be converted to a minor or dominant chord) – this will cause problems in using the new chord as an embellishment within an existing chord progression.

COMMON EMBELLISHMENTS

Perhaps surprisingly, chord embellishments are often easier to play than the basic major chords. For example, if you simply lift the finger off the first string when playing an open position D major chord shape this will convert it into a Dsus2 chord. It is called a 'sus2' chord because the open E note that will sound is the second note of the D major scale, and it replaces the third note of the scale (F♯) which has been 'suspended'. Likewise, in a 'sus 4' chord, the fourth note (G) replaces the F♯. Exercise 1 has examples of both (CD track 17).

Using sus2s and sus4s to vary the open D chord is extremely effective, and you will hear many examples in famous songs and riffs.

SIXTHS, SEVENTHS AND NINTHS

Adding an extra note to a chord is also a very effective way of creating interesting sounds. The sixth, seventh and ninth notes of the major scale all bring a certain richness and beauty when added to a basic major chord (exercises 2 & 3, CD tracks 18 & 19).

Alternating between a basic chord shape and adding or varying notes within the chord can help you create strong chordal riffs; Keith Richards was a pioneer of this style of rhythm guitar playing (exercises 4 & 5, CD tracks 20 & 21).

FURTHER VARIATIONS

It isn't just major chords that can be embellished: the same approach can be taken with minor chords by using notes from the natural minor scale with the same starting note (exercise 6, CD track 22).

The system works well for fingerpicking as well as strumming. In fact within a fingerpicked piece you can create even more opportunities for adding a wider range of scale notes to the basic chord structure (exercise 7, CD track 23).

Exercise 1: D Major Variations　　　　　⊙ 17　Backing track: ⊙ 18

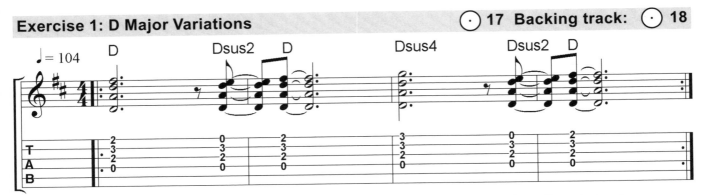

Release the second finger to create the Dsus2 chord, add the fourth finger to make a Dsus4 chord.

Exercise 2: G Major Variations　　　　　⊙ 19　Backing track: ⊙ 20

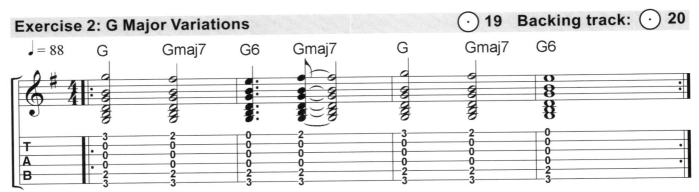

Major seventh and major sixth chords are great for ballads and can be used freely in place of the tonic major chord. In this progression, you could omit the B note on the fifth string and mute the A string instead if you prefer.

Exercise 3: C Major Variations　　　　　⊙ 21　Backing track: ⊙ 22

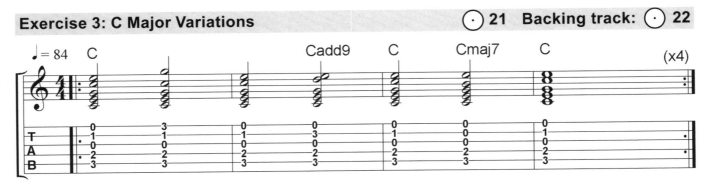

After playing the chords as notated you should try making up your own rhythm pattern using the same progression. A sample rhythm is played on the CD track after the first 8 bars. Note that you don't need to strum all of the notes of the chords.

Exercise 4: E Major Variations　　　　　⊙ 23　Backing track: ⊙ 24

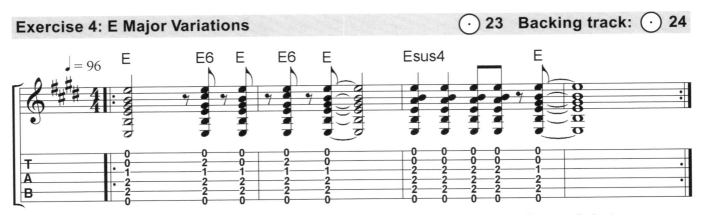

Observe the rests between chords: the crisper sound will help make this chordal riff more distinct.

Exercise 5: A Major Variations ⊙ 25 **Backing track:** ⊙ 26

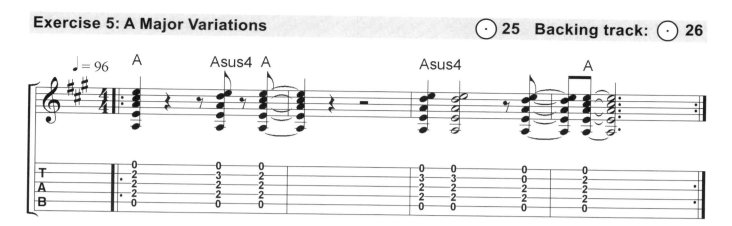

Once again, observing the silences between chords will help give this chordal riff a clear rhythmic identity.

Exercise 6: A Minor Variations ⊙ 27 **Backing track:** ⊙ 28

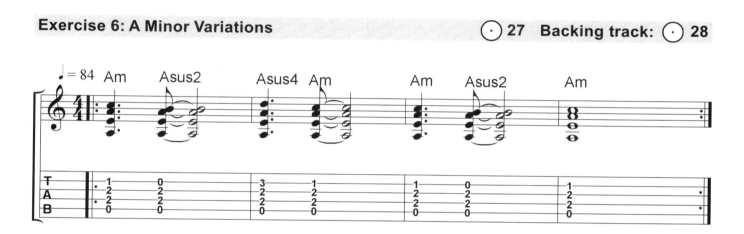

To bring out the melody line at the top of this chordal pattern try to strum down only onto the second string, i.e. avoid striking the first string.

Exercise 7: E Minor Variations ⊙ 29 **Backing track:** ⊙ 30

The open strings form the chord of E minor; all the melody notes on the first string are taken from the E natural minor scale.

BARRE CHORDS

PLAYING OPEN POSITION CHORDS IS THE PERFECT WAY TO START LEARNING THE GUITAR, BUT THE TIME EVENTUALLY COMES FOR ALL GUITARISTS TO MOVE FURTHER UP THE FINGERBOARD.

Many good rhythm players use shapes known as 'barre chords': with all six strings being held down by the first finger. Playing barre chords involves re-fingering an open position chord so as to leave the first finger free to play the barre, and then moving the whole chord up the fingerboard to different pitches. The main advantage of using barre chords is that you can move the same shape up or down the fingerboard to create new chords without the need to memorise a whole host of different fingerings for each chord. However, there are also other important benefits: barre chords allow you to play more unusual chords (like Bbm or F#) that are unobtainable in open position; and because barre chords don't involve open strings they can sound great with distortion, and you can use punchy rhythmic techniques (like staccato) more easily.

GETTING STARTED

Begin with a moveable E major shape barre chord by re-fingering an open position E major chord using the second, third and fourth fingers. Then practise moving this up to different fingerboard positions, with the first finger fretting all the strings on the adjacent lower fret. Most guitars have marker dots on frets 3, 5 and 7 and moving the barre of the E major shape to these positions will give the chords of G, A and B major. In theory, you could play all major chords with just this one barre chord shape; in practice however this would involve leaping around the fingerboard too much when changing from one chord to another. To avoid this it is necessary to know at least two shapes for each chord type: this will enable you to play through most songs without ever having to shift more than a couple of frets for each chord change.

The second major shape you can convert to a barre chord is the open position A major shape. You will find that moving this shape with the barre on the marker dots on frets 3, 5 and 7 of the A string will give the chords of C, D and E major. Both types of major barre chord are used in exercise 1 (CD tracks 31 & 32).

MINOR BARRES

Just as open position major chords can be moved up to become barre chords, so can minor chords. The E minor and A minor shapes can be re-fingered to leave the first finger free to make the barre. When the E minor shape is moved up, the pitch of the chord should be taken from the barre position on the E string. When the A minor chord is moved up, the pitch should be taken from the barre position on the A string (exercise 2, CD tracks 33 & 34).

Most songs will combine a mixture of major and minor chords. Whether you decide to use an E shape or an A shape barre chord will depend on the position of the previous and the following chord: the trick is choose the shape that will avoid any unnecessarily large fingerboard shifts (exercise 3, CD tracks 35 & 36).

Barre Chord Shapes & Fretboard Diagram

E major barre shape.

A major barre shape

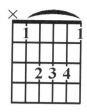

E minor barre shape

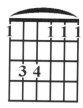

A minor barre shape

Fret	1	2	3	4	5	6	7	8	9	10	11	12
E String	F	F#/G♭	G	G#/A♭	A	A#/B♭	B	C	C#/D♭	D	D#/E♭	E
A String	A#/B♭	B	C	C#/D♭	D	D#/E♭	E	F	F#/G♭	G	G#/A♭	A

Use this table to find where chords are located on the fretboard. For example; an E major barre shape played at the third fret will produce a G major chord, and an A major shape played at the same position will produce a C major chord.

Barre Chord Technique

Don't be surprised if you find barre chords tough going at first – they are harder than open chords; however, the following tips will help minimise the difficulty:

1. Keep the first finger straight and in-line with the fret.
2. The barring finger need not be completely flat – it can be slightly tilted away from the fret toward its outer edge.
3. Position the barring finger so that the creases between its joints do not coincide with the strings and cause a string to be deadened.
4. Position all the fretting fingers as close to the fretwire as possible.
5. Press down firmly, but avoid using excessive pressure with either the first finger or with the thumb.
6. When you move between barre chords ensure that the thumb also shifts at the same time – so that your whole hand position is moving with each chord change.

Exercise 1: Major Barre Chords

⊙ 31 **Backing track:** ⊙ 32

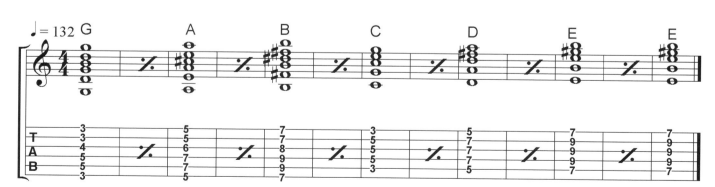

Major barre chords using E and A major shapes played on frets 3, 5 and 7. A lead riff has been included on the CD for melodic effect.

Minor barre chords using E and A minor shapes. None of these chords can be played in open position, so this type of chord progression demonstrates the necessity of learning barre chords.

Exercise 3: Mixing Major And Minor Barre Chords 35 Backing track: 36

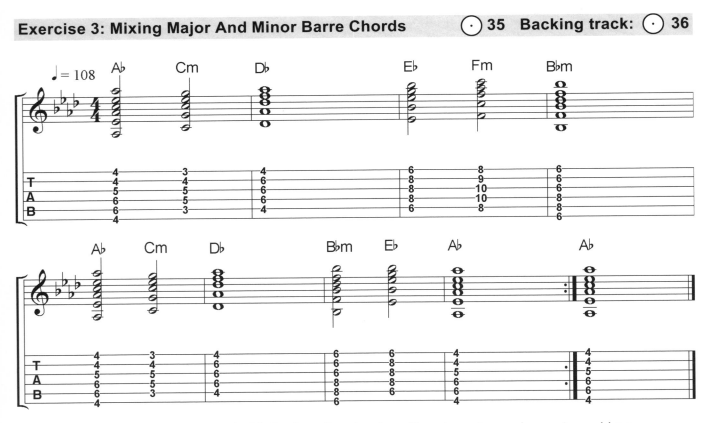

Mixing major and minor barre chords. Notice how the chord positions have been chosen to avoid any unnecessary fingerboard shifts.

MOVEABLE CHORDS

TAKING BASIC CHORD SHAPES AND MOVING THEM UP THE FINGERBOARD CAN RESULT IN SOME VERY INTERESTING CHORD SOUNDS.

The simplest way to discover new chord sounds is to experiment with moving basic chord shapes up and down the fingerboard. A good starting point is to take an open position D major chord and move it to various fret positions whilst still strumming the open D string. The D string will act as a 'pedal note' so that each chord will create a different harmonic effect when played against the D string; many interesting chord sounds can be achieved just by moving this one shape around. An example of this is shown in exercise 1 (CD tracks 37 & 38).

An extension of this technique is to move up a chord and keep not only the bass string as an open pedal note, but also some open treble strings. This technique can create some very colourful sounds. Exercise 2 is an example of moving up the basic E major chord shape to create a typically Spanish sound (CD tracks 39 & 40). Don't be put off by the complex sounding chord names that are created when chords are moved up the fingerboard – if you look closely at the tablature you will notice that the track is quite easy to play, with just the same basic E shape being moved up and down the fingerboard. A chord that has a difficult sounding name isn't necessarily difficult to play, and vice-versa. ('B' sounds easy but in fact is quite a hard chord to play, whereas Em11 can be played by simply strumming all the open strings).

MOVING BASS

When moving chords up the fingerboard you don't always need to use open bass strings as pedal notes to create unusual sounds. For example, a basic C major chord shape can be moved around, with the open third and first strings acting as the pedal notes. An example of this is shown in exercise 3 (CD tracks 41 & 42). Another variation on this technique is to move around a chord shape, including the bass note, keeping only the top two treble strings open as pedal notes. An example in this style is shown in exercise 4 (CD tracks 43 & 44).

USING MINORS

It is not only major chord shapes that can be moved up the fingerboard: the technique also works with minor chord shapes. When looking at the chord symbols this might not be immediately obvious, because when a minor chord shape is moved up the fingerboard and mixed with open strings it may end up becoming a major chord of some type. An example is shown in exercise 5 (CD tracks 45 & 46). Here, a basic A minor chord shape is moved up to create some very unique chord sounds.

As you can see from the five exercises there are innumerable chords that could be created by using these techniques. The best chord shapes to move up the fingerboard at first are D, E, C, A and Am. Experiment writing a few sequences of your own – don't worry what the chords should be called, just concentrate on how good they sound!

Fretboxes for all the chords in this lesson are on page 22.

Moving a basic D major shape, whilst keeping the open D string as the bass note, creates interesting harmonic effects.

Exercise 2: Spanish-Style Chord Movement   · 39 **Backing track:** · 40

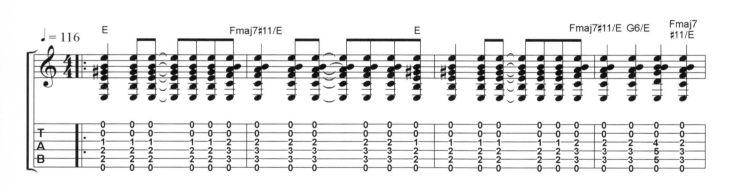

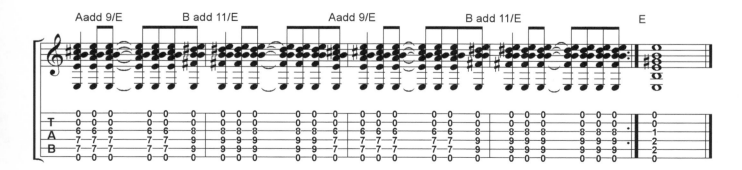

Moving an E major shape creates a Spanish flamenco type of sound.

Exercise 3: Moving The Open C Chord

⊙ 41 Backing track: ⊙ 42

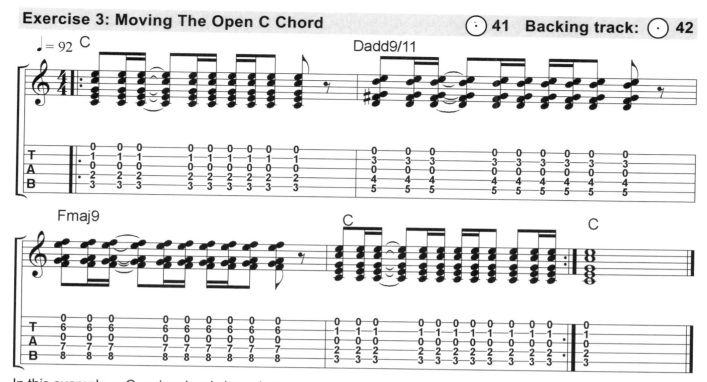

In this example, a C major chord shape is moved around the fretboard, and the harmonies created by the open third and first strings create a colourful sound.

Exercise 4: Moving Chords On The Bass Strings

⊙ 43 Backing track: ⊙ 44

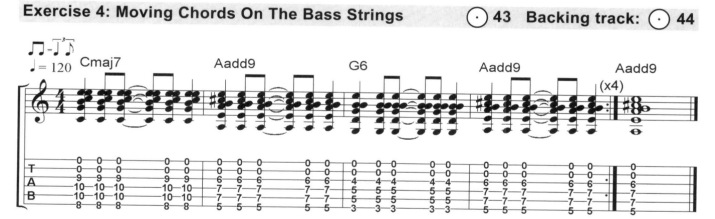

In this sequence, the open first and second strings act as pedal notes to create interesting harmonies and a jangly sound.

Exercise 5: Moving Minor Chords

⊙ 45 Backing track: ⊙ 46

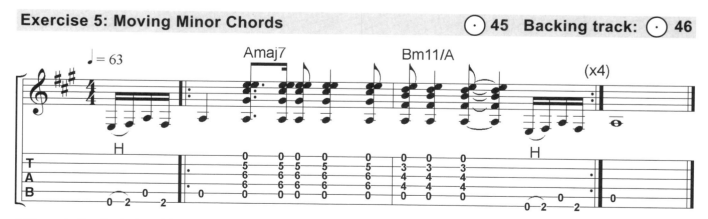

Although the first chord is a major seventh, its fingering can be derived by moving the A minor chord shape up the fretboard.

Chords Formed By Moving Open Chord Shapes

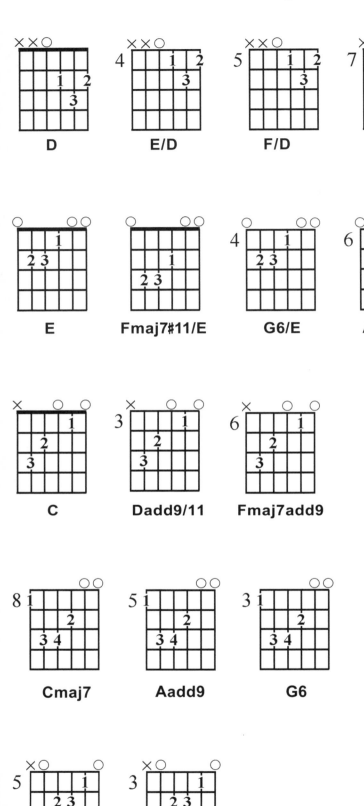

D

E/D

F/D

G/D

E

Fmaj7#11/E

G6/E

Aadd9/E

Badd11/E

C

Dadd9/11

Fmaj7add9

Cmaj7

Aadd9

G6

Amaj7

Bm11/A

SLIDING CHORDS

SLIDING CHORDS IS A USEFUL AND EFFECTIVE TECHNIQUE FOR MAKING CHORD CHANGES SOUND SMOOTHER AND MORE INTERESTING.

To 'slide' a chord means to fret it and then, whilst maintaining the fretting pressure, to move the fingering to another fret – without strumming the chord again. The second chord is sounded only because of the continued pressure of the fretting hand. The guitar is one of the few instruments on which you can slide chords up and down – changing their pitch easily and smoothly; the technique creates a fluidity and smoothness of sound that keyboard players can only dream of. Because slides are so natural to the guitar they form a core component of any good rhythm guitarist's technique. Slides are used by guitarists in nearly all musical styles, from metal and blues to country and ska.

SLIDING TECHNIQUE

Controlling the amount of grip with the fretting hand is the secret to good sliding: you should try to ensure that the thumb at the back of the guitar neck relaxes its grip when you are in the process of sliding a chord up or down. This doesn't mean that the thumb needs to be released totally, but simply that it shouldn't be squeezing tightly against the back of the guitar neck. However, just as your hand reaches the chord that you want to slide into, the thumb should squeeze the neck slightly harder to act as a brake: preventing your fingers sliding beyond the 'destination' fret. Whilst all this is happening it's important to ensure that the chord shape is maintained: so that one finger doesn't end up a fret ahead of the rest! The trick is to achieve a neutral balance whereby the chord shape is kept under control, yet at the same time the fingers are relaxed enough to slide up or down the fingerboard. If you've never tried sliding chords along the fretboard before, it's best to warm up by experimenting with sliding a few single notes around first.

UP AND DOWN

Playing fifth (power) chords, where only two notes are fretted, is the ideal introduction to sliding chords. Exercise 1 (CD tracks 47 & 48) features an example of this: first using an 'ascending slide' from two frets below the destination chord, and then using a 'double slide' (sliding down and then back up one fret). Exercise 2 (CD tracks 49 & 50) progresses onto sliding three-string major chords (triads), with the first finger fretting the top two strings. (Note that chord sliding only works easily with chords that do not contain open strings). Exercise 3 (CD tracks 51 & 52) uses three-string minor chord slides, with all the chords being fretted with only the first finger (playing a half-barre). Lastly, exercise 4 (CD tracks 53 & 54) demonstrates how sliding a major sixth chord shape around the fingerboard in a regular pattern can add real shape and character to a blues rhythm guitar part. Once you have acquired a good sliding technique you can apply it to any fretted chords – sliding into a chord from the same chord shape a fret or two either above or below.

Exercise 1: Sliding 5ths Rock Lick ⊙ 47   Backing track: ⊙ 48

It's best not to attempt the double slide in the second bar until you feel competent with the single ascending slide in bar 1.

Exercise 2: Sliding Major Triad Rock And Roll Lick ⊙ 49   Backing track: ⊙ 50

Remember to 'put on the brakes' after each slide by gripping with the thumb at the back of the neck – this will stop you overshooting the destination fret.

Exercise 3: Sliding Minor Triad Funk Lick ⊙ 51   Backing track: ⊙ 52

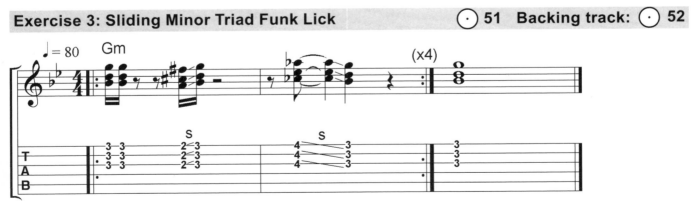

The first slide is quick and ascending, whilst the starting chord in the descending slide is held 'long' – you'll have to keep a strong pressure with the fretting finger in order to maintain the volume.

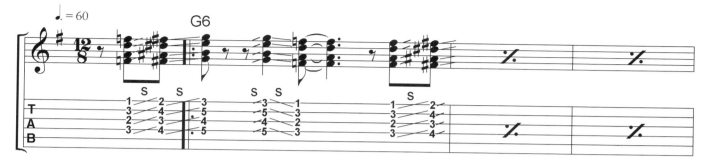

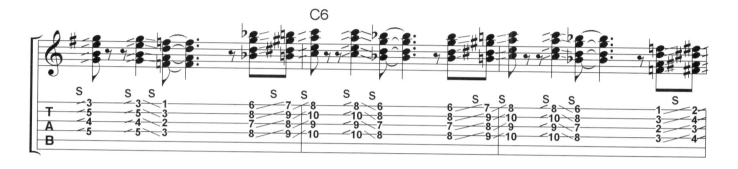

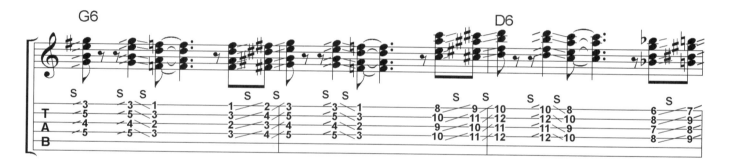

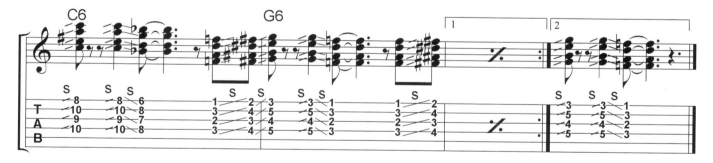

Notice how the ascending slide passes through two chords on its way to the destination chord, whereas during the descending slide the intervening chord is not emphasised.

> **Sliding Chords Tip**
>
> Playing fifth chords with a copious amount of distortion is the easiest way to begin chord sliding: the distortion will give sustain that will allow you not to have to grip too hard when sliding the chords. Using ascending slides (raising the pitch of a chord) is easier at first – the volume tends to disappear quite quickly with descending slides.

CHORD RIFFS

SOME OF THE MOST MEMORABLE RIFFS IN THE HISTORY OF ROCK MUSIC HAVE BEEN CREATED BY USING COMBINATIONS OF CHORDS RATHER THAN SINGLE NOTES.

It is often assumed that chords are used purely for strumming an accompaniment, whilst the interesting parts of songs (e.g. the main riffs or themes) have to be played using single lead lines. However, chords are in fact frequently used to create the main riffs (memorable melodic and rhythmic themes) within songs; bands as diverse as AC/DC and the White Stripes have used this technique in some of their most well-known tracks.

CREATING RIFFS

Using chords to play riffs will nearly always result in a much more powerful sound than a riff played just using single notes, so have a go at making up some chord riffs of your own.

When creating riffs with chords you'll normally need to use more than one chord per bar in order to give a sense of movement. You could start off by just strumming each chord once and then adding a more complex rhythm to the chords as the song progresses (exercise 1, CD tracks 55 & 56).

Using rests (silences) between chords will help add a more well-defined rhythm to your riff, giving it more musical shape and character (exercise 2, CD tracks 57 & 58). Another effective technique is to separate the bass and treble strings when you strum a chord – this will allow you to create an almost piano-like effect (exercise 3, CD tracks 59 & 60).

Chord riffs do not need to consist exclusively of chords: adding an occasional single note, particularly an open bass string can add variety to a riff and often makes it easier to play (exercise 4, CD tracks 61 & 62). As well as using standard chords, chord variations – particularly 'sus' chords – are ideal for using in chord riffs, as they give variety without making the chord pattern too hard to play (exercise 5, CD tracks 63 & 64).

PLAYING RIFFS

When playing chord riffs it's not always necessary to strum all of the strings – often just strumming the root, fifth and octave notes of a chord ('normally' the three lower strings of the chord) will suffice. In fact, playing these 'power chords' often actually sounds better than strumming all the strings of the complete chord shape (exercises 6 & 7, CD tracks 65-68).

Playing chord riffs will inevitably involve the need for some fast chord changes. The trick is to practise the chord changes very slowly at first – only speeding up once you are totally secure in moving between the chords. An important chord changing technique is to use the 'minimum movement principle' (discussed in depth earlier in this book): look at the similarities between chords and wherever possible try and keep any fingers in place, or at least keep them on the same string or fret; this will minimise the amount of finger movement required and will therefore reduce the amount of time taken to change between chords.

Exercise 1: Open Chord Riff   ⊙ 55   Backing track: ⊙ 56

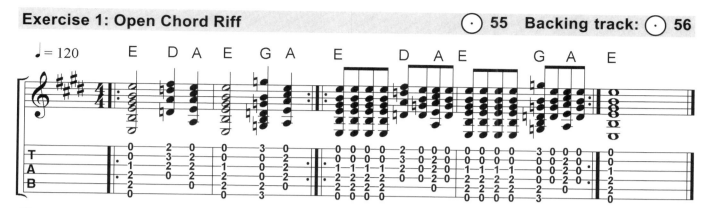

Allow the chords to ring-on in the first section of this riff. In the second section, use an upstrum to strike the open strings after the D and A chords; this 'open vamp' technique makes changing chords much easier.

Exercise 2: Chord Riff With Rests   ⊙ 57   Backing track: ⊙ 58

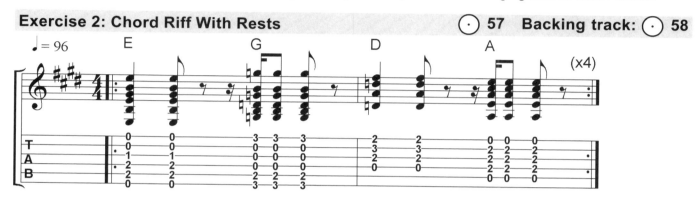

The rests give this riff its distinct rhythmic character. Observe the rests by placing the strumming hand against the strings in order to mute them.

Exercise 3: Separating Bass And Treble Strings   ⊙ 59   Backing track: ⊙ 60

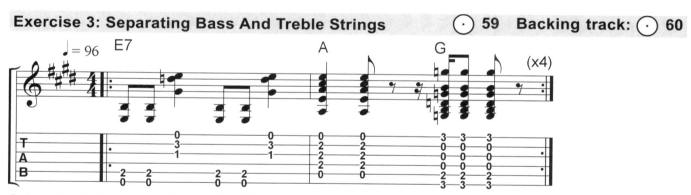

Only strike the two bass strings of the E7 chord in the first part of bar one, followed by just the treble strings of the chord. This gives more much definition to the riff than if you just strum all the strings on every chord.

Exercise 4: Chord Riff With Open E String   ⊙ 61   Backing track: ⊙ 62

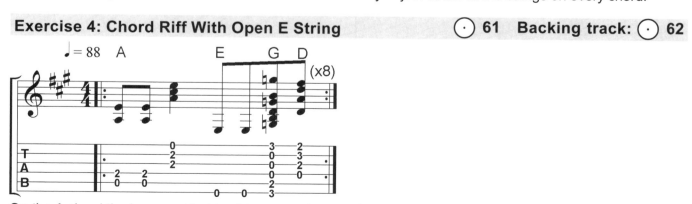

On the A chord the bass and treble strings are strummed separately. The open bass E string is then used to facilitate the change to the G chord.

Exercise 5: Riff With Sus Chord   · 63   Backing track: · 64

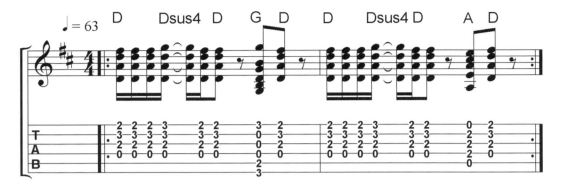

The sus4 chord adds an effective, but easy to play, variation to the D major chord. Make sure to observe the rests in the second half of each bar.

Exercise 6: Chord Riff With Fast Changes   · 65   Backing track: · 66

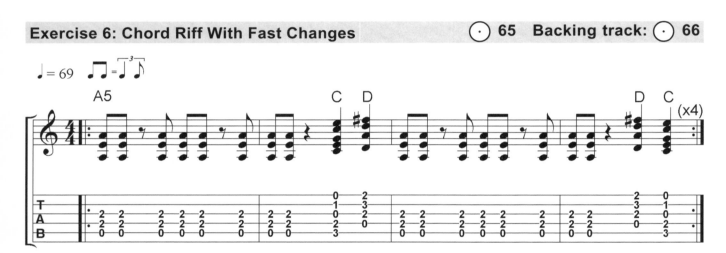

Use the A5 power chord rather than the full A major chord in this riff to create a rocky sound. In order to handle the fast chord changes between the C and D chords, notice how the 3rd finger can stay on the 3rd fret when changing between these chords.

Exercise 7: Power Chord Riff   · 67   Backing track: · 68

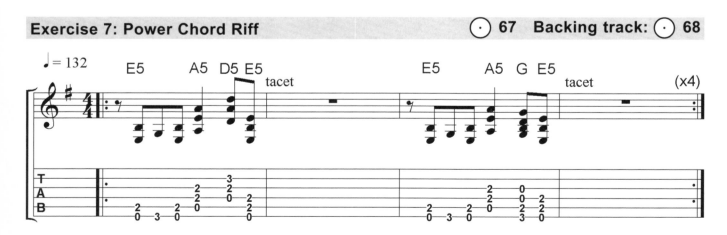

Power chords are used to give a hard rock sound. Notice how in the first part of each riff the single G bass note, rather than a G chord, is used to make the riff easier to play at speed.

CHORD LICKS

ADD A LITTLE ZEST TO YOUR RHYTHM GUITAR PLAYING WITH THE ADDITION OF A FEW CHORD LICKS.

Straightforward major chords can be made to sound much more interesting with the addition of a few simple embellishments or variations. By altering the highest note in a chord, and then resolving back to the original chord voicing, you can create small melodic licks as part of your rhythm playing. This sort of rhythm playing can be used in all styles of music: rock players from Keith Richards to Noel Gallagher use these techniques; but it's particularly suited to soul and funk styles – whose classic exponents include Nile Rodgers and Steve Cropper. As these chord licks are just variations of the main chords, they are often not written out above the notation. However, fretboxes of the chords used in this lesson are provided on page 32.

CHORD VARIATIONS

The first example (exercise 1, CD Track 69) focuses on the use of add ninth chords – a chord type much favoured by rhythm maestro Steve Cropper (who played with Otis Redding, Booker T and the MGs, and featured in the Blues Brothers films). You can work out other 'add nine' chords by adding the ninth note of the relevant major scale to any major chord. For example, add the note of D to a C major chord to make Cadd9. (The ninth note of each major scale also happens to be the same as the second note of the scale – remembering this will save you having to count so far up the scale!)

The secret of Cropper's excellent rhythm guitar style is based on his adage: "It's not so much what you play – as what you *don't* play". Rather than filling all the beats of a bar with relentless strumming, Cropper tends to accent only certain beats – so that a 'groove' is set-up. That way his playing always interacts well with what the drums and bass are playing. Get a feel for this technique by listening to the demo track, and playing along to the backing track (CD track 70). It is not necessary to keep the rhythm exactly the same as on the recording – adding subtle variations (as the recording does in the repeat section) is extremely common in rhythm playing.

MORE ADDITIONS

Exercises 2 - 4 illustrate three shorter rhythm ideas. The first of these (exercise 2, CD track 71) is based on major seventh chords, but with the 6th (or maj13) and #4 (or #11) notes added to create melodic variations. The classic soul fusion ballad 'Midnight At The Oasis' uses this style of chord lick. The next example (exercise 3, CD track 72) features sus4 chords – often used in soul, but equally at home in rock, folk and numerous other styles. The final example (exercise 4, CD track 73), incorporates open strings to create sus2 chords – these are similar in construction to add9 chords, except that the third of the chord is missing. Compare them to the chords in the main demo track and you should be able to hear the difference.

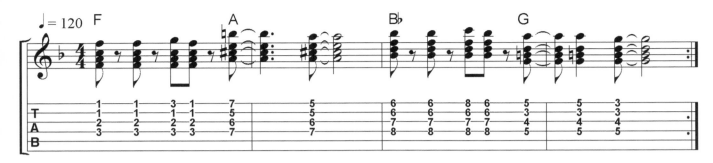

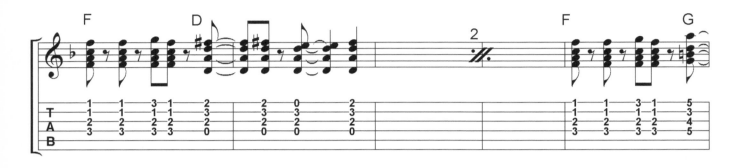

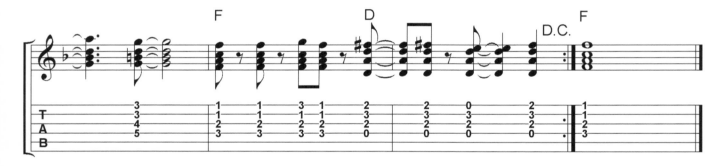

On all these chords you should only strum the first four strings – this gives a thin crisp sound that is highly suited to soul and funk styles. Make sure that you don't strum any open bass strings as this would totally ruin the effect.

Exercise 2: Major 7ᵗʰ Chord Licks ☉ **71**

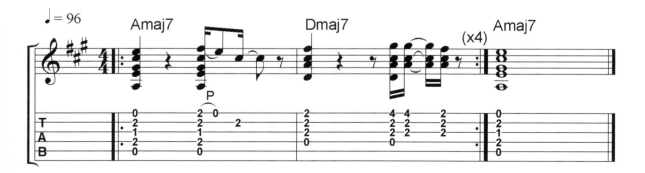

Embellishments based on major 7ᵗʰ chords.

Exercise 3: Sus4 Chord Licks

72

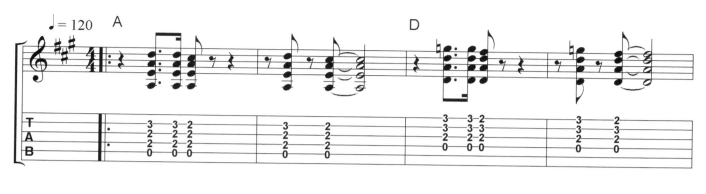

Each bar starts with a sus4 chord before resolving to a major chord.

Exercise 4: Sus2 Chord Licks

73

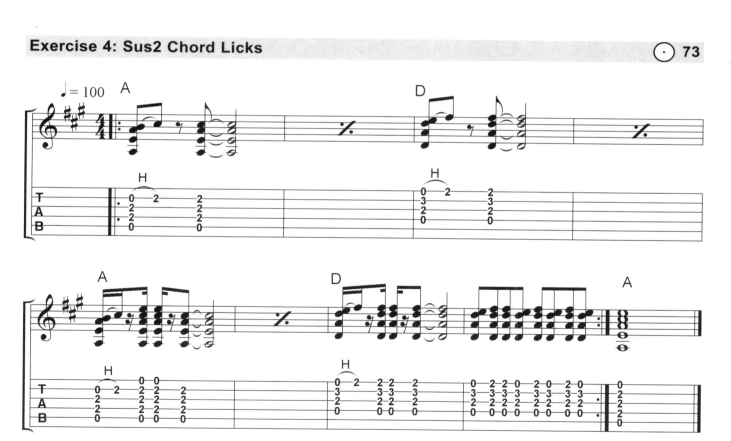

Each bar starts with a sus2 chord before resolving to a major chord. Notice how the last four bars are variations on the first four.

LESSON EIGHT – CHORD LICKS

31

Chord Shapes Used In Lesson 8

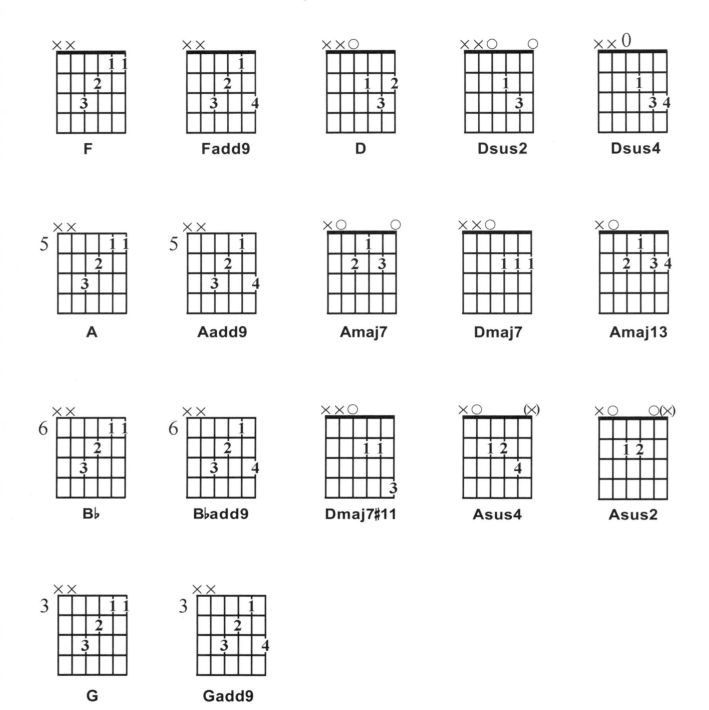

Notice that for some of the chords you need to fret more than one string with your first finger. This technique is called a 'half-barre' – it requires you to press with the pad of the first finger rather than on the tip.

REGGAE & SKA RHYTHMS

ALTHOUGH BOTH REGGAE AND SKA RHYTHMS WERE ORIGINALLY CONFINED TO JAMAICAN ROOTS MUSIC, THEIR INFLUENCE HAS NOW SPREAD ACROSS MANY DIFFERENT MUSICAL STYLES.

Ska was developed from the Caribbean musical traditions of calypso, blue beat and mento. The most dominant musical force in ska was Prince Buster, who influenced successful ska bands such as The Upsetters and The Skalites. In the late 1960s, Jamaican musicians such as Bob Marley and the Wailers, and Toots and the Maytalls, took the rhythmic characteristics of ska but slowed down the tempos and gave the music a more soulful mood to create reggae.

The late 1970s saw a resurgence of ska music, with two-tone bands like Madness and The Specials adding a punk-influenced rawness to the music. Reggae was also adapted by British bands, such as UB40 and The Police, with huge commercial success.

PLAYING THE BACKBEATS

Listen to any reggae song and you will notice how prominent the bassline is. The guitar's role is to add regular chord chops which, through their repetitive rhythm, serve to emphasise the melodic movement of the bass. In the purest form of reggae, the guitar part is limited to a single downstrum on the second and fourth beats of the bar, i.e. strumming only on the 'backbeats' rather than the main beats of the bar (exercise 1, CD tracks 74 & 75). This might take a little getting used to if you've never played reggae before. A good tip is to listen to the bass, as this often plays on the first beat of the bar, and establish your rhythm just after the bass has begun. It's important that you keep an even, steady beat, because the guitar is acting as an essential part of the rhythm section.

To get the short, crisp guitar sound that is used in reggae and ska, chords must be played 'staccato', often striking only the top three or four strings: immediately after each strum you must mute the strings by resting your strumming hand against them; you can also slightly release the pressure with the fretting hand to prevent the chords ringing-on.

OTHER RHYTHMS

In some styles of reggae a downstrum is played four times a bar, on the 'off-beats' – this is known as 'single skank' style (exercise 2, CD tracks 76 & 77). This method is occasionally followed by a quick upstrum to create a 'double skank' (exercise 3, CD tracks 78 & 79).

Some players even mix single and double skanks within a song (exercise 4, CD tracks 80 & 81).

Ska rhythm usually involves playing on all four off-beats. It differs from reggae, not only in the faster tempo that is often used, but in that chords are normally played with upward strums. Examples of ska rhythms can be found in exercises 5-7 (CD tracks 82-87).

Exercise 1: 'Two Drop' Reggae Rhythm   ⊙ 74   Backing track: ⊙ 75

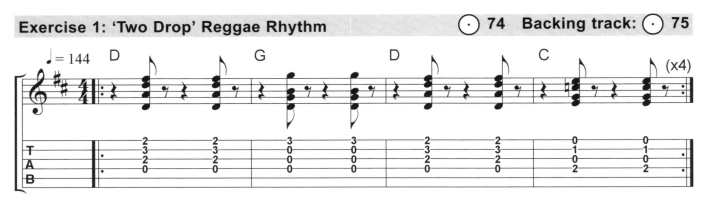

Play a single downstroke on beats two and four. Notice that you don't need to strum all of the strings in each chord; playing just the top four strings will give a crisper sound.

Exercise 2: 'Four-Drop' Reggae Rhythm   ⊙ 76   Backing track: ⊙ 77

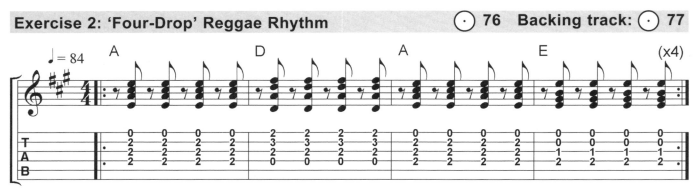

Play four staccato downstrokes – each on the 'off-beat'. Try to keep a constant regular rhythm throughout.

Exercise 3: 'Double Skank' Reggae Rhythm   ⊙ 78   Backing track: ⊙ 79

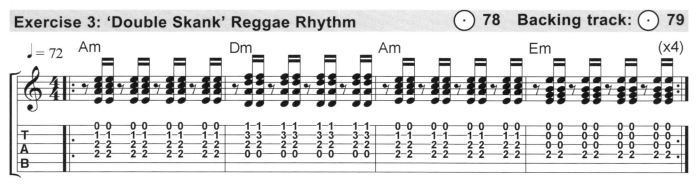

After each downstroke immediately 'bounce back' with an upstroke across the treble strings. You only need to strike the top three treble strings – particularly on the upstrokes.

Exercise 4: Mixing Single And Double Skanks   ⊙ 80   Backing track: ⊙ 81

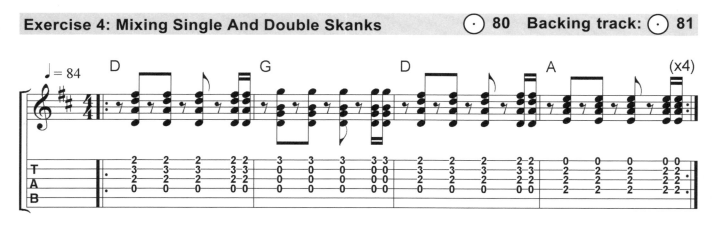

Play the first three strums of each bar with a downstoke. The 16th notes at the end of each bar should be played by a downstroke rapidly followed by an upstroke.

Exercise 5: Ska Rhythm

● 82   Backing track: ● 83

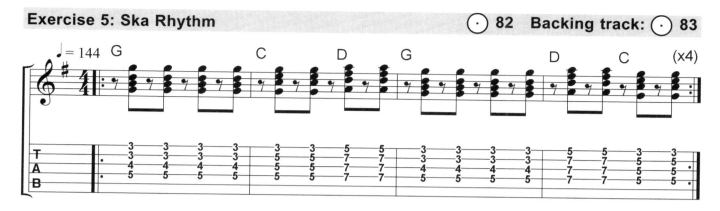

This fast and repetitive off-beat strumming style requires a flexible wrist action, so that the upstrums stem from the wrist and not from movement of the arm.

Exercise 6: Ska Rhythm With Slides

● 84   Backing track: ● 85

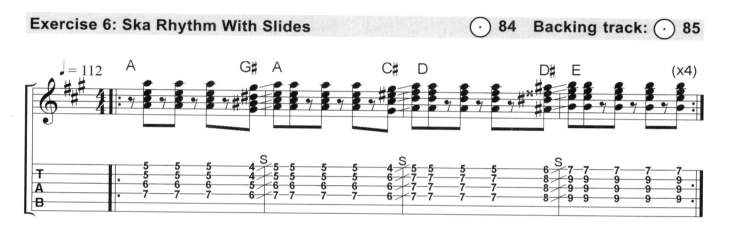

This rhythm features a slide from a chord one fret below the target chord. This technique is often used in ska as a way of varying the rhythm.

Exercise 7: Ska Rhythm Variation

● 86   Backing track: ● 87

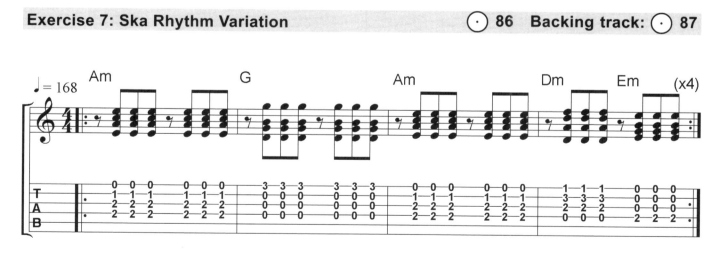

This rhythm uses an up/down/up rhythm pattern, creating an interesting alternative to the standard off-beat rhythm. Bands like Madness often used this pattern in their ska-based music.

SPANISH RHYTHMS

THE GUITAR WILL ALWAYS BE ASSOCIATED WITH SPAIN – LEARN HOW TO ADD A SPANISH FEEL TO YOUR OWN PLAYING.

Latin music has become extremely popular in recent years, and the rhythmic and melodic elements of this style can be easily incorporated into your own playing. Most Latin music can be traced directly back to the traditional gypsy guitar music of the Andalucia region of Southern Spain. The Moors, who came from North Africa and invaded southern Spain in the 15th century, left a very distinctive and exotic influence on Spanish music which has remained to this day. Their influence is most prominent in the guitar style known as flamenco.

FLAMENCO TECHNIQUES

The term 'flamenco' literally means to impress and dazzle, and all flamenco strumming patterns are based on exuberant traditional dance rhythms. Three examples of typical Spanish rhythms are given in exercises 1-3 (CD tracks 88-90). It is best to play these fingerstyle, as several bars contain an essential flamenco strumming technique known as 'rasqueados'. To achieve this effect, strum the strings by releasing the first three fingers in quick succession – so that the fingers rapidly roll across the strings one after another. However, if you are using a plectrum you can achieve a very similar effect by playing a 'half-circle' strum: on an acoustic guitar start at the middle of the soundhole and as you strum downwards trace the outline of the soundhole in a single movement with the plectrum; first moving towards the bridge and then back towards the neck – tracing a half-circle shape. (If you have an electric guitar then simply strum your half-circle shape around the middle pick-up.)

A SPANISH PIECE

The demonstration piece, *'Andalusian Sunrise'*, (CD track 91) is similar to the form of a lively Spanish dance known as 'Soleares'. Although it is superficially based in the key of A minor, the dominant chord of E major provides the fundamental harmonic role. The backing sequence consists of the chord sequences within exercises 1 to 3 played 'seque', (i.e. continuously without a break). Notice how all the sequences begin and end with the chord of E major.

SPANISH LEAD

After learning all these new rhythm techniques, it is time to play some lead. The first 16 bars of the melody have been notated in fig 4 as they appear on the CD. After this follows 12 bars of improvisation using the E Phrygian modal scale. Don't be put off by the complex sounding name of this scale - it simply consists of the notes of the A natural minor scale from E to E (E, F, G, A, B, C, D, E). Use the backing track (CD track 92) to practice the melody and to try out your own improvisations. If you want to get a really Spanish sound you can occasionally alter the G note to become a G♯ – as this note is contained within the E major chord. Playing this note will bring out the Moorish influence in the music. Both scales are notated at the end of the lesson.

Exercise 1: Spanish Rhythm No.1

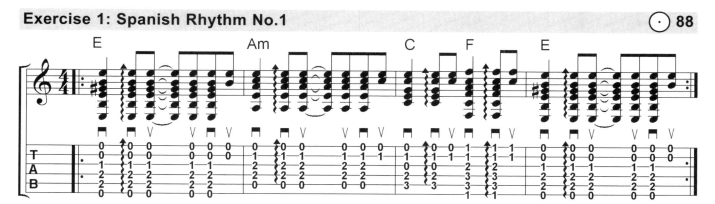

The wavy line next to some of the chords indicates that you should use a rasqueado strum.

Exercise 2: Spanish Rhythm No.2

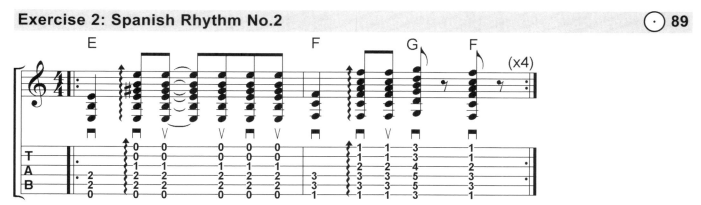

It will be easier to change to the barre chord shapes for F and G if you finger the E major chord without using the first finger.

Exercise 3: Spanish Rhythm No.3

Don't be scared by the Fmaj7#11 chord in bar 2 - it's just an F major chord with the first two strings played open! The variations on the E and F chords in the remaining bars are typical of flamenco music – the E chord occasionally contains an F note (hinting at the F chord that is about to come), whilst the F chord occasionally contains E and B notes (harking back to the E chord that has just gone).

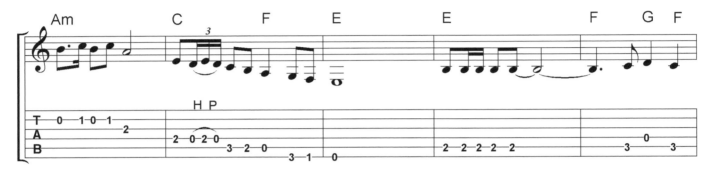

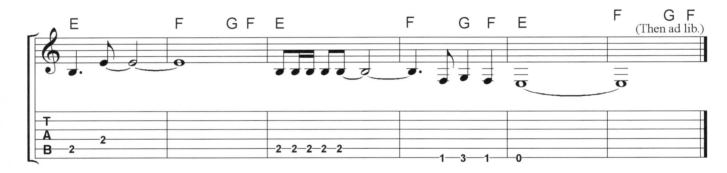

Andalusian Sunrise, as featured on CD track 91. This melody comes from the E Phrygian modal scale. The final section (which is not notated) features the same scale used for improvising.

Spanish Scales

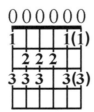

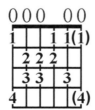

E Phrygian modal scale. Use this scale to improvise over the backing track.

E Phrygian-major modal scale. To get a real Spanish flavour, over the E major chords, you can change all the G notes in the standard Phrygian scale to G#.

Chord Shapes

Below are the open position chord shapes that are used in this book. Remember, however, that the mark of a competent rhythm guitarist is not only knowing the chords, but also being able to change between them fluently.

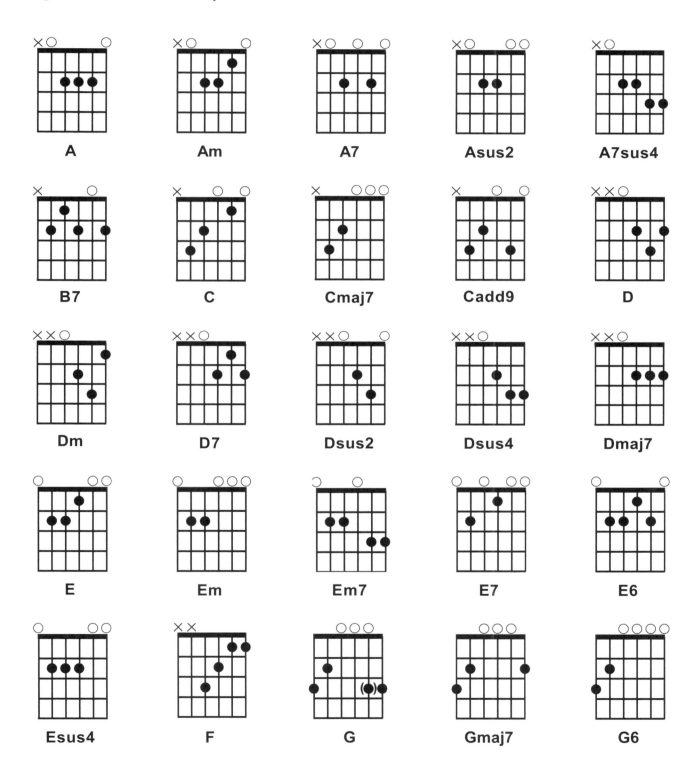